# ZAKKA HOME

## 19 MODERN & STYLISH PROJECTS FOR YOUR HOME

SEDEF IMER

T0366370

**Tuva Publishing**

www.tuvapublishing.com

**Address** Merkez Mah. Cavusbasi Cad. No:71
Cekmekoy - Istanbul 34782 / Turkey
Tel: +9 0216 642 62 62

**Zakka Home**

**First Print**  2018 / September

All Global Copyrights Belong To
Tuva Tekstil ve Yayıncılık Ltd.

**Content** Sewing

**Editor in Chief** Ayhan DEMİRPEHLİVAN

**Project Editor** Kader DEMİRPEHLİVAN

**Designer** Sedef IMER

**Technical Editors** Leyla ARAS, Büşra ESER

**Graphic Designers** Ömer ALP, Abdullah BAYRAKÇI, Zilal ÖNEL

**Photograph** Tuva Publishing, Sedef IMER

**Illustrations** Murat Tanhu YILMAZ

**ISBN** 978-605-9192-38-5

# CONTENTS

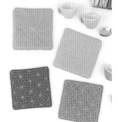

# PREFACE

In Japanese the word 'Zakka' literally means 'many things', 'sundries', or simply put, 'stuff'! During Japan's post war economic boom it was typically used to describe everyday mundane objects. The use of the phrase has evolved over the decades – today 'Zakka' describes a design aesthetic that combines usefulness with beauty and style. If a mundane, everyday object is made with love and gives you joy and happiness – it's Zakka!

In this book I have lovingly created a collection of simple, pretty, and handy projects inspired by the art of Zakka to help organize and beautify your home. I'm a complete homebody myself – there is nowhere I'm happier than when I'm at home, with my family. So it goes without saying that sewing things for my home is really what I enjoy doing the most. This book contains many different types of projects, all with different uses inside your home – I hope you enjoy sewing them as much as I did designing them. And most importantly, I hope they bring you joy.

Zakka Home continues my journey as a sewing author which started with the publication of my first book, Quilt Petite, which was all about mini quilts and small quilty things. Whilst quilting and patchwork remains at the heart of what I do, especially in my patterns and fabric collections, I also enjoy a challenge – and writing Zakka Home was just that, pushing me out of my 'comfort zone'. I am entirely self-taught as a sewist, having only learned to sew in 2012 – so writing this book was a very rewarding experience and has greatly expanded my sewing repertoire. All projects in this book are very 'doable' and suitable for all levels of sewists – if you've never tried a particular method, go ahead, just 'give it a go' – that's my sewing motto!

*Sedef Imer*

# PROJECT GALLERY

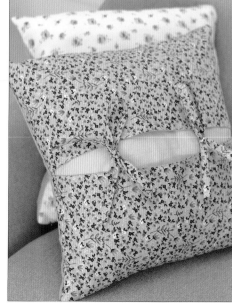

# MY FAVOURITE TOOLS

# MY FAVOURITE TOOLS

These are the tools I use every day, and couldn't live without! It's definitely worth investing in good quality tools that will give you better results and stand the test of time. All of the tools I use are available in good craft and quilting stores.

- My sewing machine is a Janome Memorycraft 7700 QCP which has an extra-wide throat (handy for quilting) and a wide range of feet for different applications. The two feet that I use most often are my walking foot, and the ¼" foot.

- I use a smoothing spray such as Flatter or Best Press to prepare my fabric for cutting.

- For cutting I use a large self-healing cutting mat, my trusty Olfa 45mm rotary cutter, and Kai professional scissors.

- Pins & Needles. I use ultra-thin Clover patchwork pins for all my patchwork, long plastic headed pins for general use, and curved quilting pins to baste the layers of a quilt together before quilting. I recently invested in a set of Tulip Hiroshima needles which come in different sizes and thicknesses for different applications - I would never go back to using ordinary needles again. They glide through fabric like a hot knife through butter and make hand sewing so much more pleasurable.

- Threads. I use Aurifil thread for sewing, DMC floss for embroidery, and DMC Perle Cotton No:8 for hand quilting.

- Fabric markers. I use either my Pilot Frixion pens (which come in a range of colours and disappear when pressed with a hot iron) or my Clover Hera marker. The Pilot Frixion pens are great, but the lines can reappear when exposed to cold, so I use those when the traced lines will be hidden inside the project or to trace embroidery patterns. To mark quilting lines on a quilt top I use the Hera marker.

- Fabric glue pen. I use it for English paper piecing and also for quickly basting two pieces of fabric together.

- Clover seam ripper. Most sewing machines come with a basic seam ripper but it's worth investing in a good one as they provide much better results when unpicking a seam.

- Quilting clips. These purpose made clips hold several layers of fabric together without leaving a mark on them. I use them when I'm sewing the binding on to a quilt, or when I'm blind stitching an opening to close it.

- Non-slip quilting rulers. I have quite a large collection of these, in varying sizes and shapes. A recent addition that has quickly become a favourite is my Bloc Loc ruler which is a must if you work with half square triangles a lot.

- Quilting gloves. These gloves have a grippy material on the finger tips which makes moving your project on the sewing machine so much easier, thus reducing hand and shoulder fatigue. They also help keep your hands and your project clean!

# TECHNIQUES

## 1. PATCHWORK PRECISION TIPS

Some of the projects in this book assume a basic level of knowledge of patchworking. If you are a complete beginner, I highly recommend taking a craft class or checking out online video tutorials to learn the basic principles. Here are a few additional tips to improve the precision of your patchwork projects.

Always starch your fabric before you cut. I use a spray starch and spray it lightly onto the fabric (without soaking it), then press with a medium hot dry iron (no steam) until the fabric is dry. Make sure the iron is not too hot or the starch may scorch, leaving stains on your fabric. Also note that we are using the term 'press' rather than 'iron' – it's important that you only apply vertical pressure and no sideways pressure or the fabric may stretch and distort.

When cutting fabrics, use a self-healing cutting mat and good quality non-slip quilting rulers. Change your rotary cutter blades frequently – blunt blades will chew and stretch your fabric as you cut.

Pin blocks together well before sewing, especially at junctions - the more pins you use, the more precise your work will be.

Invest in a 1/4 inch presser foot, as it makes it so much easier to get that precise quarter inch seam, which is the standard seam allowance for patchwork.

Press seams that will intersect in opposite directions so you can 'nest' or 'butt' the seams against each other when you are sewing the two pieces together. I pin the nesting seams together using a single pin placed at a slight angle - push the pin down through one seam, and back up again through the other seam.

Check sizes of pieced blocks before continuing on to the next step.

# 2. EMBROIDERY

## 1. RUNNING STITCH

This is one of the most basic embroidery stitches, and is achieved by running the needle and thread in and out of the fabric at even intervals. The key to an attractive running stitch is keeping both the stitch length and the interval length consistent across the entire line of stitching, on both sides of the fabric. Bring the needle up at 1, then down at 2, then up at 3, down at 4, and continue.

## 2. BACK STITCH

Like the running stitch, the backstitch creates a line made up of straight stitches, but without any spaces between the stitches. Bring the needle up at 1, down at 2, up again at 3, down at 1, and continue.

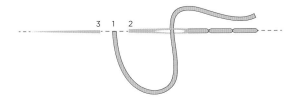

## 3. FRENCH KNOT

This is a very simple knot in principle but may take a little practice to get right. Bring the needle up through the fabric. Holding the thread taut with one hand, wrap the thread twice around the needle. Push the needle down into the fabric just next to the original hole, still holding the thread taut. Pull the thread through to the backside until a knot is formed.

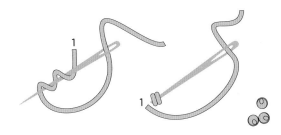

## 4. LAZY DAISY STITCH

Commonly used to make flower petals or leaves. Bring the needle up at A, then push it down right next to A and bring it out at B, looping the thread under the needle (tip: don't pull the thread too taut if you want nicely rounded petals rather than thin ones). To anchor the stitch, push the needle down just on the other side of the loop.

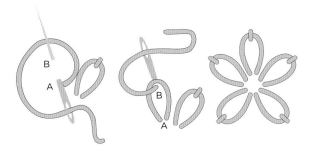

## 5. FISHBONE STITCH

Commonly used to make leaves. Bring the needle up at A, along the central 'spine' of the leaf. Down at B, up again at C and down at D, slightly overlapping the previous stitch. Up again at E and continue in this manner. Make sure your stitches are right next to each other so that there are no gaps, and maintain the angles of the stitches uniform.

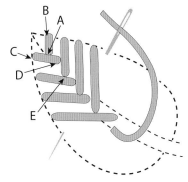

## 6. ROSETTE STITCH

Also known as the 'woven wheel stitch', this stitch is used to make roses. Bring the needle up at the centre of your rose and make five straight stitches at equal intervals – these will be the 'spokes' of the wheel. Bring the needle up at the centre again and begin weaving the needles over and under each spoke. You may want to use a blunt needle such as a tapestry needle for this. Continue weaving the thread over and under the spokes until the rose shape is completely filled.

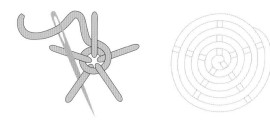

## 7. SPLIT STITCH

Make a small stitch about the length of a large grain of rice. Next, bring your needle up through the centre of the stitch you just made, and make another stitch the same length as the first one. Continue in this manner. This super simple stitch is a great alternative to back stitch.

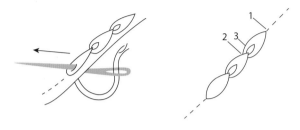

## 8. SATIN STITCH

This is a series of flat stitches that are parallel to each other and used to completely cover a defined area. Bring up the needle at 1, and down again at 2 to make a long stitch. Come up again right next to 1 and down again right next to 2. Continue in this manner, following the outline of the shape you are embroidering. Keep your stitches neat and parallel to each other so the surface of the area you are filling looks smooth.

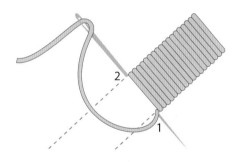

## 9. LONG AND SHORT STITCH

This is another stitch used to fill a defined area, especially when the area in question is too big for satin stitch or to create colour shading. Start by stitching a row of alternating long and short stiches. Then work a second row of long stitches aligned with the short stitches of the first row. Continue in this manner changing the colour of the thread as required.

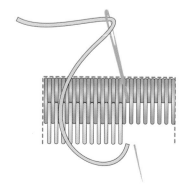

# 3. APPLIQUE

## 1. RAW EDGE APPLIQUE WITH FUSIBLE WEB

- Cut a piece of fabric slightly bigger than your applique template shape, and a piece of fusible web the same size as your fabric.

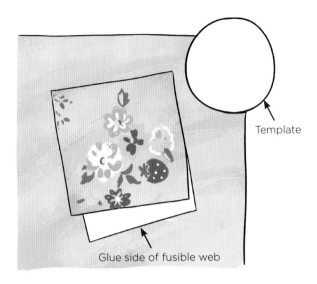

Template

Glue side of fusible web

- Place the fusible web on the wrong side of your fabric, glue side facing the fabric. Press with hot iron (no steam) for five seconds or so until they are fused together.

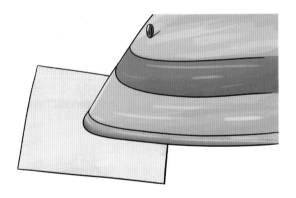

- Place the applique template on top of the paper backing, and trace around it with a pen. Pay attention to the orientation of the shape so you don't end up with a mirror image.

- Cut the shape out along the traced line. Peel off the backing paper, place on top of your backing fabric, and fuse in place with a hot iron.

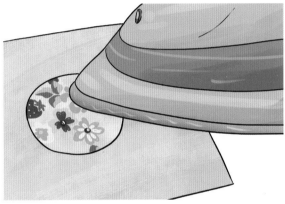

- Using a very short stitch length on your machine stitch all the way around the shape, as close to the raw edge as you can get (1-2mm). Secure your beginning and end stitches well.

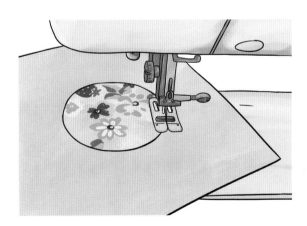

## 2. APPLIQUE WITH FUSIBLE INTERFACING

- Cut a piece of fabric slightly bigger than your applique template shape, and a piece of fusible lightweight interfacing the same size.

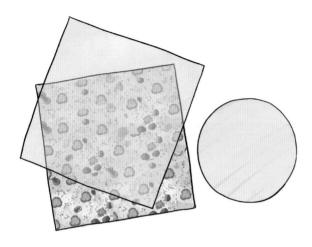

- Place the right side of the fabric against the fusible (shiny) side of the interfacing. Place the applique template on the back of the interfacing, and trace around it.

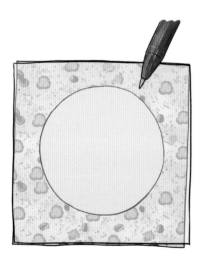

Stitch all the way along the traced line.

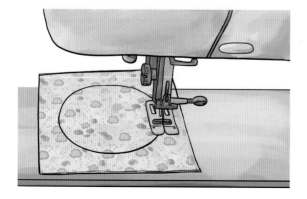

Using pinking shears trim off the excess fabric and interfacing. Cut two perpendicular slits on the back of the interfacing using sharp scissors, taking care not to get too close to your stitches. Turn the fabric inside out through the slits, and using a thin blunt object such as a chopstick push out the edges of the fabric until the shape is smooth and even.

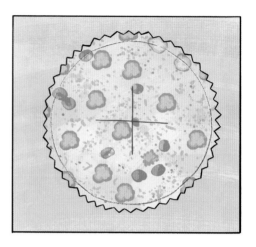

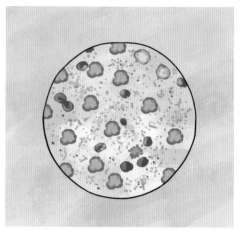

Place on top of the background fabric and press with hot iron to fuse the shape onto the background. Applique the shape to the background using tiny stitches either by hand or by machine – your stitches should be right at the edge of the applique shape and 2-3mm apart.

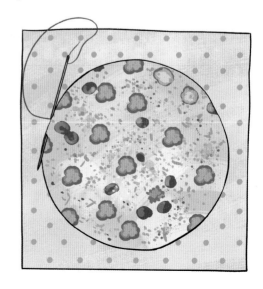

# 4. QUILTING

The four stages of making a quilt are: 1. Making the quilt top, 2. Making a quilt sandwich, 3. Quilting (by hand or machine) and 4. Binding.

## MAKING A QUILT SANDWICH

Quilts and small quilted projects typically consist of three layers – the patchwork quilt top, the batting in the middle, and the backing.

To make a quilt sandwich lay your quilt backing on a flat surface, right side facing down. Place the batting on top, then the quilt top, facing right side up. Baste together with curved quilting pins, starting at the centre and moving outwards. Use lots of pins, and when finished check that the backing is smooth without any big wrinkles or folds.

## QUILTING

The next step in the process is to stitch the three layers together, either by hand or by machine.

### 1. HAND QUILTING

I use hand quilting a lot in my work as I love the vintage crinkly feel it gives my finished projects. Hand quilting is simply that – it's a running stitch done by hand so can be quite time consuming for large quilts! For all my hand quilting I use DMC Perle Cotton No:8. Make sure you 'bury' your knots if you use this method – to bury a knot simply tug on the thread until the knot pops through the backing fabric into the wadding.

### 2. STRAIGHT LINE QUILTING

This is the simplest quilting to perform on a domestic sewing machine with a walking foot – you can do vertical, horizontal or diagonal lines at regular or varying intervals, lots of parallel lines close together (known as matchstick quilting), lines criss-crossing each other to create a checker or diamond effect – the possibilities are endless!
A commonly used technique when straight line quilting is to stitch-in-the-ditch – this is when your quilting line lies in the seam between two adjacent patchwork pieces, and is almost invisible.

### 3. FREE MOTION QUILTING

This is also performed on a domestic sewing machine, but instead of the walking foot you use an open toe or darning foot with the feed dogs dropped down (so the quilt can move freely in the machine). Stippling is a popular free motion design, you can also do pebbles, spirals, leaves, or clamshells, to list a few. I highly recommend using a pair of non-slip quilting gloves for free motion quilting – they allow you to control the movement of the quilt a lot more precisely.

### 4. LONG ARM QUILTING

You can also get your quilting done by a professional long arm quilter, who have specialist machines with big frames, and offer a great variety of wonderful quilting patterns that you can select from. The only drawback of this option is the cost, especially for smaller quilts, as there is often a minimum charge.

# BINDING

Binding is one of my favourite parts of the whole quilt making process as it means I am on the home stretch! You can buy pre-made bias tape at most craft stores but I prefer to make my own as it gives me more choice in terms of fabrics. I almost always cut my binding cross grain (ie straight strips, from selvedge to selvedge) as this wastes the least amount of fabric – the only exception is if the quilt I am binding has curved edges (in which case I use bias binding, ie. cut on a 45 degree angle from the selvedge - cross grain binding does not give sufficient stretch for curves). I also like my binding quite narrow so I cut all my binding strips 2 ¼" wide. If you prefer thicker binding you can adjust this to your personal preference.

## 1. BINDING WITH MITRED CORNERS

- You first need to make continuous binding that is approximately 10" longer than the circumference of your quilt. For most projects this will require piecing together at least two or more strips of binding to make one long piece. To do this, place two strips right sides together and at a right angle to each other. Draw a 45 degree line as shown, sew on the line, then trim the excess fabric ¼" away from the stitching. Press the seam open to reduce bulk. Repeat adding more strips until you have the desired length of binding.

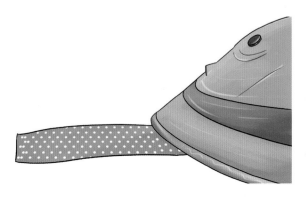

Place the binding on top of the quilt, right side of the quilt facing up and raw edges aligned, and with the start of the binding placed roughly around the middle of one edge of the quilt. Pin along the length. When you get to a corner place a pin at a 45 degree angle, flip the binding up at a right angle (with the raw edge aligned with the next edge of the quilt), then fold it back down again. Pin.

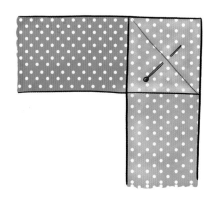

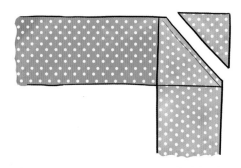

Fold the binding in half lengthwise, wrong sides together, and press.

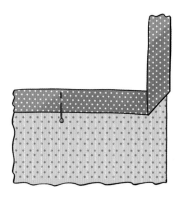

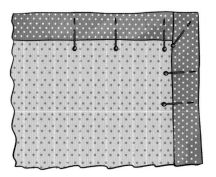

Leaving a 5" 'tail' at the beginning of the binding start sewing a ¼" seam along the length. When you get to the corner stop sewing ¼" away from the edge. Pull the quilt out of the machine a little (you don't have to cut your thread), flip the corner up as shown, and starting on the next side ¼" from the corner sew a ¼" seam along the length again. Repeat all the way around the quilt until you are approximately 10" away from the starting point of the binding.

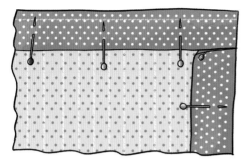

Trim the two tails of binding so they overlap by the exact width of the binding (in my case 2 ¼" as that's the standard width for all my binding). Sew the two ends together at right angles as described in the first step above. Press the seam open, then finish sewing the binding on to the quilt.

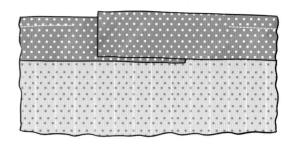

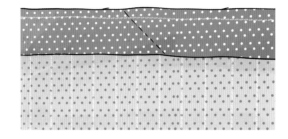

Fold the binding strip over to the back of the quilt, and place quilting clips all the way around to keep the binding in place. Hand stitch the bottom edge of the binding to the back of the quilt as shown, sewing a few extra stitches on the corners the quilt.

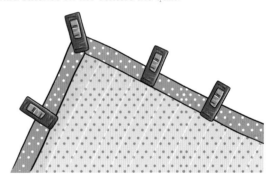

## 2. BINDING CURVES

For curves it is essential to use binding strips cut on the bias (ie at a 45 degree angle to the selvedge) as straight grain binding does not stretch well enough over curves.

The binding method is exactly the same as explained above, except pin the curves as shown, with lots of little folds.

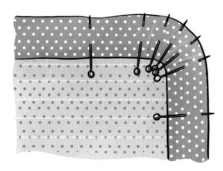

something
GOOD

# ARMCHAIR CADDY

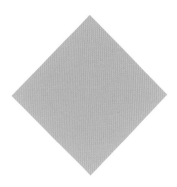

If like me you like to craft on the couch from time to
time, you will appreciate this useful caddy to keep all
your pins, scissors, and other crafting items nearby.
Pack it all away in a jiffy at the end of your session to
keep them out of the way and keep little oncs safe.

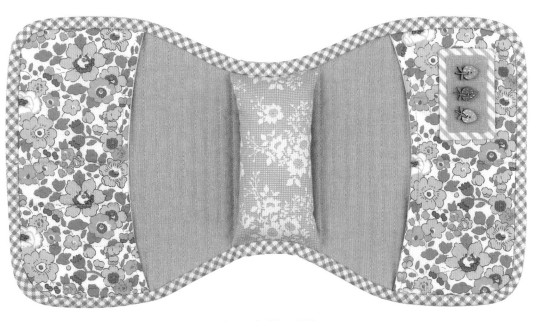

Size: 8.5" x 16"

## MATERIALS

(2) 10" x 18" grey cotton (background & backing)

(1) 10" x 18" batting (caddy)

(2) 5" x 10" floral fabric (pocket outer)

(2) 5" x 10" white cotton (pocket lining)

(2) 5" x 10" batting (pocket)

(2) 1 ¾" x 2 ¾" grey (decorative tag)

(2) 2 ¼" x 3 ¼" stripy (decorative tag)

(1) 6" square floral fabric (pincushion)

(1) 2 ¼" x 60" bias gingham (binding)

Decorative buttons

Fibre fill

# STEPS

1 Copy the two parts of the caddy template and tape together. Trace it onto the right side of one of the pieces of grey cotton.

2 Make a quilt sandwich with the background fabric (right side down), then the caddy batting, and finally the grey cotton from previous step (right side facing up). Pin together and quilt in straight parallel lines 3/8" apart. Cut along the traced line to trim excess fabric and batting.

3 Trace the pocket template on the back of the two white pocket lining pieces.

4 Place one of the pocket batting pieces on the table, then the pocket floral on top (right side facing up), and finally the white cotton (wrong side with the tracing facing up). Pin or glue baste the three layers together and carefully cut out all three layers along the traced line. Sew the curved edge with a ¼" seam, open the seam and fold over to the other side, press. Top stitch the curved edge. Repeat for the other pocket.

5 Mark the centre line on each pocket. On one of the pockets mark three lines spaced 1 ¼" apart (you can skip this step if you would like two large pockets instead or size your pockets to suit your needs).

6 Prepare the decorative tag. Place the grey fabrics RST and stitch all the way around with ¼" seam. Clip the excess fabric on the corners. Make a + shaped slit on the back of one side and turn inside out through the slit. Push out the corners with a blunt instrument and press. Repeat for the stripy piece.

7 Sew the grey label onto the stripy label with tiny invisible hand stitches. Sew on the decorative buttons. Place the label at the centre of the right section of one of the pockets and hand sew in place with invisible stitches.

8 Place the pockets at either end of the caddy and pin. Baste in place with a 1/8" seam all the way around the two sides and the bottom. Sew the central line on both pockets and the three additional lines on one pocket piece, making sure you reinforce the top of the stitch lines by going back and forth a few times.

9 Fold the pincushion fabric in half right sides together and sew along the raw edge to make a tube. Press the seam open, turn inside out. Place the tube in the middle of the caddy base (seam facing down so it's not visible), pin in place, and trim off any excess fabric sticking outside the edge of the caddy. Turn upside down and sew along one edge with a 1/8" seam. Stuff the pincushion through the other side, then sew that edge with a 1/8" seam to seal the pincushion closed.

10 Press the binding strip in half lengthways, wrong sides facing together. Bind the caddy, using pins to gently ease the binding around the curved edge (see 'Techniques' for guidance on binding).

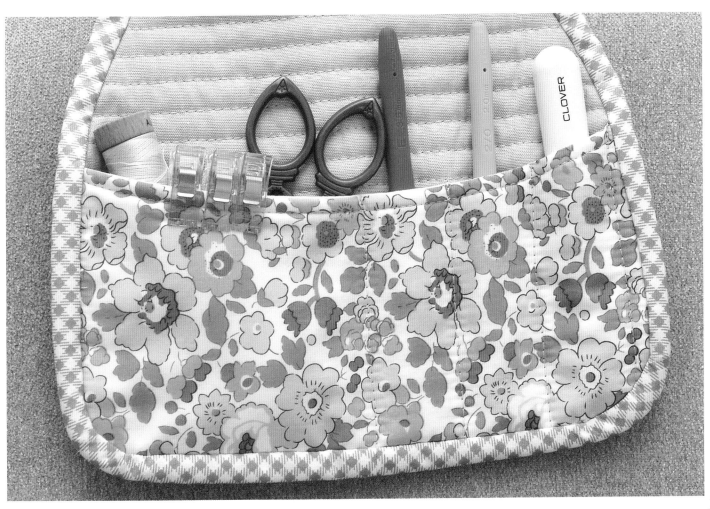

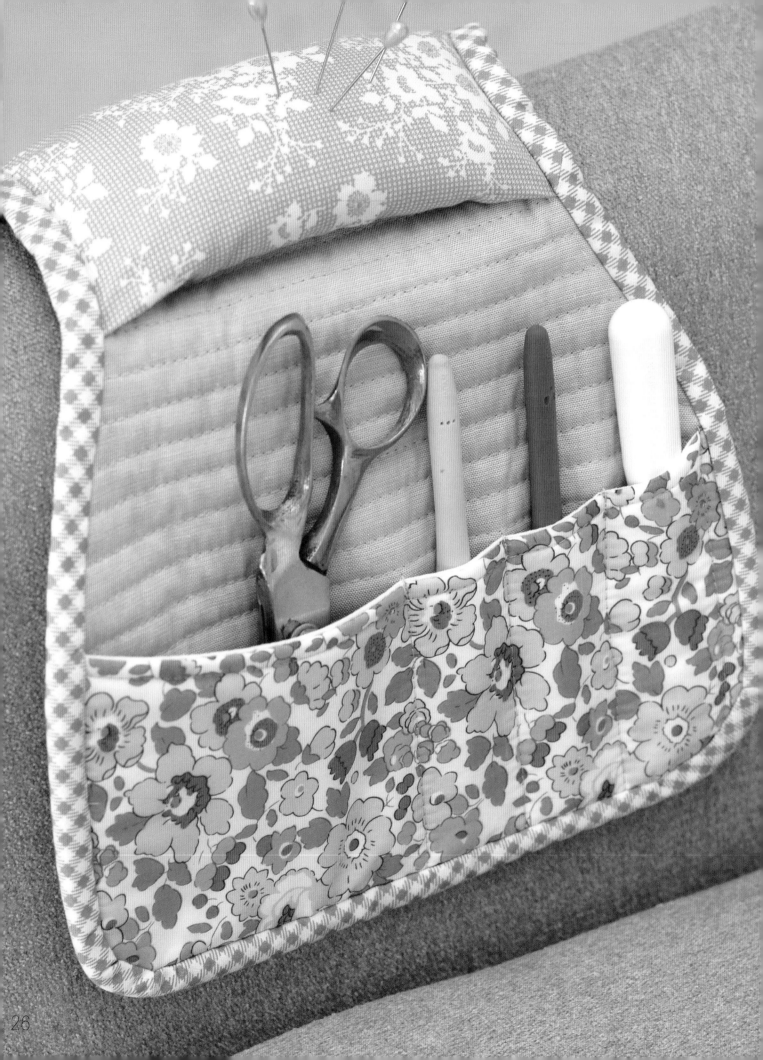

# BOUQUET EMBROIDERY

Add your own interpretation to this floral embroidery by customising the colours to suit your décor - every bouquet tells a different story.

Size: 6" diameter

Finished size: 6" diameter

RST means right sides together

Use a ¼" seam allowance unless otherwise stated

# MATERIALS

(1) 6" embroidery hoop

(1) 10" x 10" low volume fabric (embroidery background)

(1) 7" x 7" white felt (backing) – cut a 6" circle using the hoop as your template

(4) ¾" x 18" strip (hoop binding)

DMC embroidery floss in 989 (light green), 3345 (dark green), 964 (aqua), 3849 (teal), 3809 (petrol blue), 967 (peach), 3706 (pink), Blanc.

DMC Pearl Cotton Variations 4110 (variegated pink & white) (you can use DMC Cotton Perle No 8 in pink as a substitute)

All purpose glue

# STEPS

1 Using a window or light box trace the embroidery pattern onto the centre of the background fabric.

2 Stretch the background fabric onto the hoop and embroider the pattern following the stitching guide below. Refer to 'Techniques' for guidance on individual stitches.

**Small Leaves** Backstitch in 989 (3 strands), straight stitch in the centres in Blanc (3 strands)

**Large Leaves** Fishbone stitch in 3345 (4 strands), straight stitch randomly for highlights in 989 (3 strands)

**Stems** Backstitch in 989 (4 strands)

**Rose** Rosette stitch in DMC Pearl Cotton 4110, French knots in Blanc (3 strands)

**Aqua Flower** Outline the flower with split stitch in 964 (3 strands), fill with long & short stitch in 964, 3809, 3849 (2 strands) (tip: fill one petal at a time, sewing the centre stitch first then working to the right and left until it's filled), French knots in 967 (3 strands)

**Pink Flower** Outline with split stitch in 967 (3 strands), fill with long & short in 967 and blanc (2 strands), French knots in 3706 (4 strands)

**4-Leaf Clovers** Outline with split stitch in 3809 (3 strands), fill with satin stitch in 3809 (2 strands), French knots in 967 (4 strands)

**Tulips** Outline with split stitch in 3706 (3 strands), fill with satin stitch in 3706 (2 strands), French knots in Blanc (3 strands)

**Lazy Daisies** – petals in 964 (3 strands) and French knots in 967 (3 strands)

3 Remove the embroidery from the hoop to bind the outer hoop with fabric. Start by putting a small amount of glue on the inside edge of the hoop, just underneath the screw. Press the edge of the first binding strip onto the glue to secure it and then start wrapping the strip around the hoop at regular intervals. When you come to the end of strip, trim it so that the raw edge lies on the inside of the hoop (where it won't be visible), and glue it down. To start the next strip add a little more glue to the inside edge, and start wrapping again. Continue in this manner until the whole hoop is covered. Carefully snip off any frayed threads.

4 Place the inner embroidery hoop in the middle of the white felt, trace around the outside. Cut the white felt circle out along the line.

5 Place the embroidery back into the hoop and stretch. Cut off excess fabric to leave a 2" circular allowance all the way around at the back. Cut a long piece of thread (longer than the circumference of the hoop), knot at one end, and make regular stitches of the same length all the way around near the edge of the fabric. Tighten the thread to 'gather' the fabric, knot and trim the thread.

6 Run a small amount of glue around the outer edges of the felt circle and push it into the back of the embroidery. Hold in place until it's fused to the fabric.

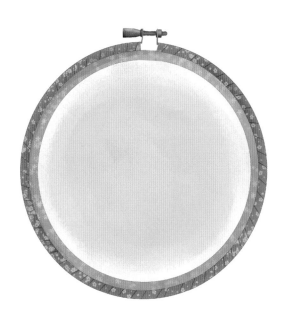

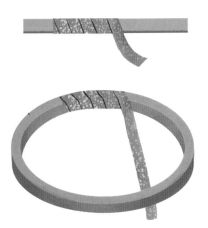

# HOUSE LAVENDER SACHETS

Who doesn't like the lovely calming scent of lavender? Hang these sachets on hangers in your wardrobe to make your clothing smell divine. They have an opening at the back so you can refill the lavender when the scent fades.

Size: 3" x 4 ½" (excluding string)

# MATERIALS

(2) 2 ¾" x 4" print fabric (roof)

(2) 1 ½" x 2" print fabric (house walls)

(1) 2" x 3 ½" print fabric (house walls)

(1) 1 ½" x 2" low volume fabric (door)

(2) 3 1/2" x 3 ¾" backing fabric

(1) 9" garden string

1 decorative wooden bead

Pearl snap for the back closure (optional)

# STEPS

**1** Trace two copies of the roof template onto the roof fabric and cut out along the lines.

**2** Place one of the small wall fabrics RST with the door fabric, sew along one long edge. Sew the other wall fabric to the other side of the door. Press seams open.

**3** Sew the large wall fabric to the top. Press open.

**4** Sew the roof to the top. Press open.

**5** Take one piece of backing fabric. Fold one of the 3 ½" edges in by ¾", wrong sides together. Press. Fold in again by another ¾". Press. Top stitch along the folded edge. Repeat for the other backing piece.

**6** Sew a roof piece to the raw 3 ½" edge of one of the backing fabrics. Press the seam open.

**7** Fold the garden string into two. Place on the tip of the roof on the front side of the house with only a little of the two raw ends sticking out and the loop pointing towards the middle of the house. Baste in place with a few stitches very close to the edge.

**8** Place the house front down on the table, right side facing up. Place the backing piece with the roof on top, right side facing down, aligning the roofs. Then place the other backing piece, right side facing down, aligning the bottom edge of the house. Pin together, making sure the seams where the roof fabric meets the other fabrics are well aligned. Sew all the way around with a ¼" seam.

**9** Turn inside out through the opening. Mark the centre point of the two hemmed edges and following manufacturer's instructions install a pearl snap here (Note: this is optional - the overlap at the opening is large enough that the lavender should not spill out without the snap).

**10** Push the string loop through the centre of a wooden bead and make a knot at the top of the bead. Fill the sachet with dried lavender buds.

37

# RUFFLED
# KITCHEN TOWEL

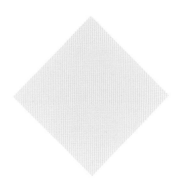

A well-made tea towel lasts so much longer than shop bought ones – I added some sweet ruffles to these ones so they are not only functional but also pretty to look at. The kitchen is the heart of the home after all!

 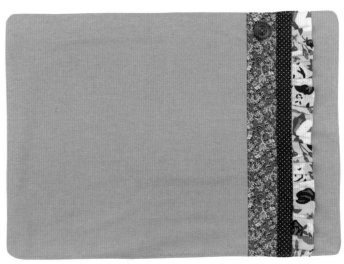

Size: 14 ½" x 20 ½"

# NOTES

Finished size: 14 ½" x 20 ½"

RST means right sides together

Use a ¼" seam allowance unless otherwise stated

# MATERIALS

To make one kitchen towel:

(1) 15" x 15 ¼" linen or solid cotton (A)

(1) 2 ¾" x 15" linen or solid cotton (B)

(1) 4" x 15" print fabric (strip with button - C)

(1) 2 ¼" x 15" print fabric (strip above the ruffle - D)

(1) 4" x 25" print fabric (ruffles)

(1) 15" x 21" print fabric (backing)

Wood button

# STEPS

1 Place A and C RST and sew together along their 15" edge. Press the seam towards C. Sew B on the other side of C, press seam open. Top stitch the seam between A and C.

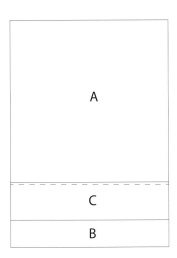

2 Make the ruffle. Fold the ruffle strip in half lengthwise with wrong sides together and press. Set your sewing machine to its longest stitch length and sew a straight line 3/8" from the raw edge all along the length of the strip. Leave at least 3" of thread tails on both ends, knot the tails at one end. Tug on the top thread at the unknotted end to bunch up the fabric slowly along the whole length of the strip. Keep doing this slowly, gently pushing the bunched fabric down until you end up with a ruffled strip 15" wide, with evenly distributed ruffles.

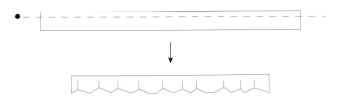

3 Baste the ruffle onto the towel along its top edge, 1/8" away from the raw edge, and leaving a 2" gap between the bottom edge of the ruffle and the bottom edge of the kitchen towel.

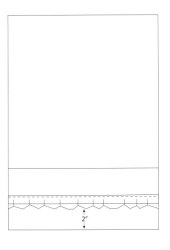

4 Fold one long edge of the D strip in by ½", wrong sides facing, and press. Repeat for the other long edge. Place it on the top edge of the ruffle, overlapping the ruffle by ¼", pin. Top stitch the top and bottom edge of the strip all the way across.

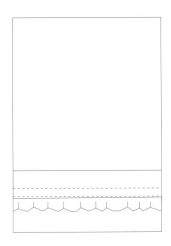

5 Place the towel top RST with the backing and pin together. Sew all the way around with a ¼" seam, leaving a 2" gap on one side. Clip the corners and turn inside out through the gap. Poke out the corners with a blunt instrument and press, carefully tucking in the seam allowance at the gap so it's even with the rest of the edge. Top stitch all the way around (this will also close the gap).

# P E G   B A G

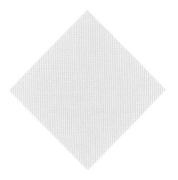

I believe clothes smell like sunshine when dried on a clothesline, the old fashioned way. Make it an even more pleasurable experience with this deliciously feminine peg bag that you can hang on the line!

Size: 10"x 12.5"

# NOTES

Finished size: 10"x 12.5"

RST means right sides together

Use a ¼" seam allowance unless otherwise stated

# MATERIALS

(1) 7 ½" x 11" floral fabric (pocket front)

(1) 7 ½" x 11" beige fabric (pocket lining)

(1) 11" x 13" dotted fabric (front)

(2) 7" x 11" beige fabric (backing)

(1) 4" x 18" pink fabric (ruffles)

(1) 1 ¾" x 10" strip (pocket binding)

(1) 2 ½" square beige fabric (hanging tab)

(1) 11" x 13" batting

Lobster clip with 1" loop

# STEPS

1 Trace the part 1 template onto the pocket front and lining fabrics. Cut both out on the traced line. Pin them wrong sides together and sew all the way around with a 1/8" allowance to baste the two fabrics together.

2 Make the ruffle. Fold the pink ruffle strip in half lengthwise with wrong sides together and press. Set your sewing machine to its longest stitch length and sew a straight line 3/8" from the raw edge all along the length of the strip. Leave at least 3" of thread tails on both ends, knot the tails at one end. Tug on the top thread at the unknotted end to bunch up the fabric slowly along the whole length of the strip. Keep doing this slowly, gently pushing the bunched fabric down until you end up with a ruffled strip 9" wide, with evenly distributed ruffles. Make sure the outer ½" on both sides of the strip is smooth with no ruffles (so they don't get in the way when we construct the peg bag later). Place on the top edge of the pocket from the previous step and baste in place with 1/8" allowance.

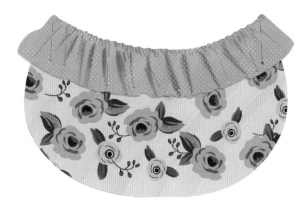

3 Fold one long edge of the binding fabric in by 1/4" (wrong sides together) and press. Fold in by another ¼" and press. Place the other (raw) edge of the binding strip on top of the ruffled pocket, right sides facing and raw edges aligned. Sew all the way around with a 1/4" seam (Note: you will have a little excess binding sticking out on both sides). Fold the binding over to the other side, hold in place with quilting clips. Blind stitch the back of the binding by hand. Trim off any excess ruffle and binding sticking out on both sides.

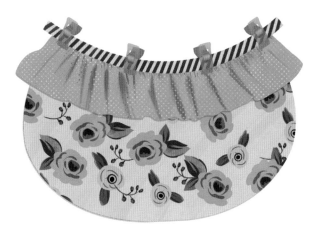

4 Place the dotted fabric on top of the batting, pin together. Quilt as desired.

5 Tape part 1 and part 2 of the template together. Place it in the middle of the quilted panel, trace around. Cut along the traced line.

6 Place the pocket on the quilted panel and baste in place around the bottom curved edge with a 1/8" seam.

7 Make the hanging tab. Fold the 2 ½ " square beige fabric in half, wrong sides together, and sew along the raw edge. Press the seam open, and turn inside out. Press. Thread it through the lobster clip, place on the top edge with the clip pointing towards the centre of the bag. Baste in place with a 1/8" seam.

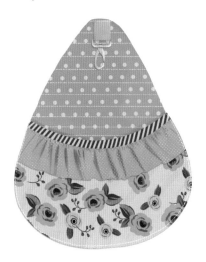

8 Sew the two backing fabric pieces together along one long edge, leaving a 5" gap in the middle unsewn. Press the seam open. Place the template on top and trace around, making sure the seam in the middle is level. Cut along the traced line. Place on top of the peg bag front, right sides facing. Pin together around the perimeter.

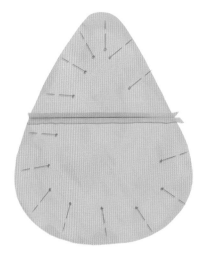

9 Sew all the way around. Turn the bag inside out through the opening in the back. Blind stitch the opening closed by hand. Top stitch all the way around 3/8 " away from the edge.

# RUCHED
# CUSHION

I'm a big believer that less is more, and the elegant simplicity of this cushion is a true case in point. The low volume floral backing acts as a counterpoint to the plain colour of the cushion front and livens up the overall design.

Size: 16" x 16"

# MATERIALS

(4) 4 ½" x 22" pink cotton (front panels)

(2) 12" x 16 1/2"" (backing)

16" cushion insert

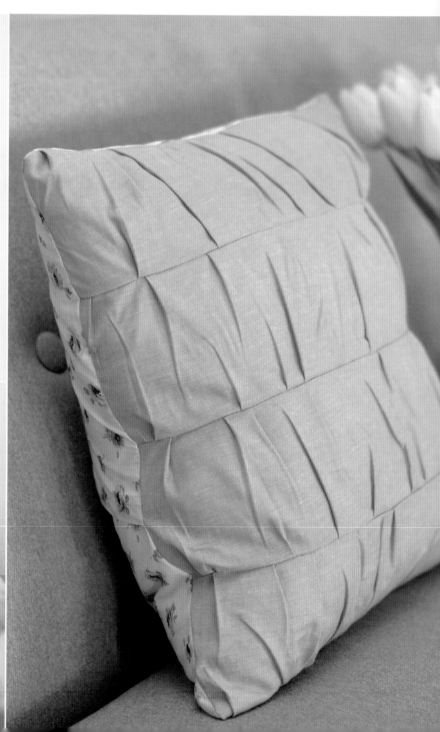

# STEPS

1 Take one of the front panels and sew along one long edge, making random folds every 1-2 inches as you sew – try to make some of the folds right next to each other for a more random look. The more folds you make, the more heavily ruched the cushion will be. When you finish sewing the edge the panel will be curved.

2 Repeat the process on the other long edge, making sure some of the folds span the whole width of the panel. When you are finished the panel should even out in shape and measure 17-18" long. We will trim this down to the required size in the next step so you don't need to be overly precise.

3 Repeat steps 1 and 2 to make four ruched panels. Sew these together along their long edges, press seams open. Trim the cushion front to 16 ½" square.

4 Take a backing piece and fold one long edge in by ½", press. Fold in by another ½" and press. Top stitch along both edges. Repeat for the other backing piece.

5 Place the cushion front on a table, right side facing up. Place a backing piece on top, right side down, raw edges aligned at the top and the folded edge towards the centre. Place the other backing piece on top, right side down, raw edges aligned at the bottom and the folded edge towards the centre. Stitch all the way around with a ¼" seam. Clip the corners and turn inside out through the opening. Poke the corners out with a blunt instrument and place the cushion insert inside.

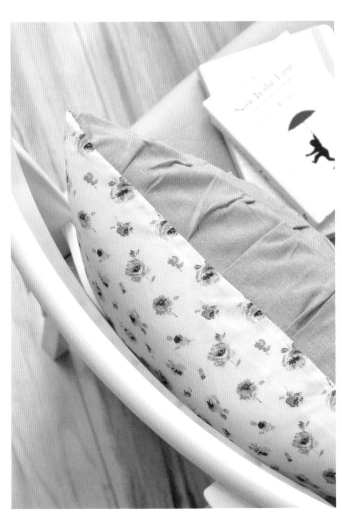

# SASHIKO COASTERS

Sashiko is a striking embroidery technique originating from Japan - its name means 'little stabs' in Japanese, referring to the plain running stitch used to create geometric repeating patterns.

Front

Back

Size: 5" square

# NOTES

Finished size: 5" square
RST means right sides together
Use a 1/4" seam allowance unless otherwise stated

# MATERIALS

(4) 6 ½" x 6 ½" solid cotton in assorted colours

(4) 5 ½" x 5 ½" floral prints in assorted colours coordinating with the solids

(4) 6 ½" x 6 ½" thick batting (or two layers of regular batting)

Sashiko thread (or DMC Perle Cotton No 8 as a substitute)

# STEPS

To make one coaster:

1 Trace the pattern template onto the centre of the solid cotton square. Place a batting square underneath, pin or glue baste together. Embroider the pattern using a running stitch.

2 Trim ½ " away from the outer embroidered square all the way around – you should end up with an embroidered square that is 5 ½" x 5 ½".

3 Place the floral square on top of the embroidered square, right sides facing. Sew all the way around with ¼" seam, leaving a 2" gap along one edge to turn inside out. Clip the corners with pinking shears. Turn inside out, blind stitch the gap closed by hand. Press.

Repeat the process to make four coasters (using a different pattern for each coaster).

# SCALLOP TRIVET

Call it a trivet, a snack mat, a candle mat, a mug rug, or a large coaster - you will find so many different uses for this sweet mini - quilt in your home!

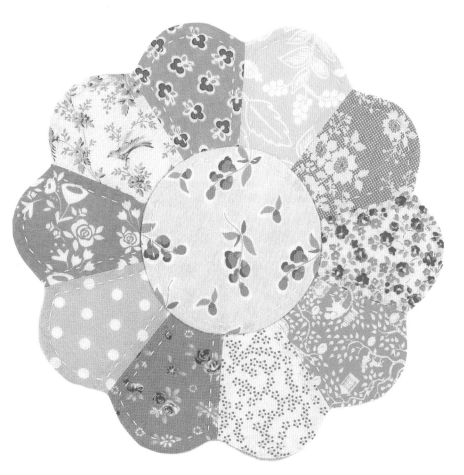

Size: 9 ½" diameter

Finished size: 9 ½" diameter

RST means right sides together

Use a ¼" seam allowance unless otherwise stated

# MATERIALS

(10) 4" x 5" rectangles in assorted fabrics

(1) 11" x 11" base fabric

(1) 11"x 11" batting

(1) 5" x 5" floral fabric for the centre

(1) 5" x 5" lightweight interfacing

DMC Perle Cotton No 8 (white) for hand quilting

# STEPS

1 Trace the trivet template onto the back of the 4" x 5" rectangles. Cut the wedges out along the traced lines.

2 Take two pieces and sew them together along one long edge with a ¼" seam. Continue in this manner sewing one piece at a time and sew the 10th piece and the 1st piece together to form a full circle as shown. Press seams open.

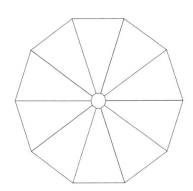

3 Place the trivet top on a flat surface with the wrong side facing up. Place the scallop template onto each 'slice' and trace with fabric pen around the curved edge.

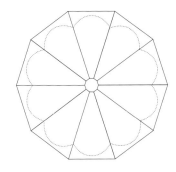

4 Make a quilt sandwich with batting, backing fabric (right side up), and trivet top (right side down), pin together. Sew all the way around along the traced scallop shape. Trim excess fabric with pinking scissors and turn inside out through gap in the middle. Push the edges out with a blunt instrument or turning tool. Press.

5 Make the central circle using the interface applique method (see Techniques). Trace the centre template onto the back of the 5" square fabric. Place on top of the interfacing square and sew all the way around on the line. Trim off excess fabric with pinking shears. Carefully cut a + shaped slit on the back of the interfacing, turn the shape inside out through the slit, push out the edges with a blunt instrument, and press. Applique in the middle of the trivet by hand or by machine.

6 Quilt your trivet by hand using a running stitch (see Techniques).

# CUSHION
# WITH TIES

I love a stylish cushion, especially when it's simple and quick to sew - and even better if it's pink and floral! The simple design of this cushion really allows the pretty floral fabric to shine.

Size: 16" x 16"

## NOTES

Finished size: 16" x 16"

RST means right sides together

Use a ¼" seam allowance unless otherwise stated

# MATERIALS

(2) 8 ½" x 16 ½" pink floral fabric (cushion front)

(4) 1 ½" x 14" strips of pink floral fabric (ties)

(2) 8 ½" x 16 ½" pink cotton (lining)

(1) 16 ½" x 16 ½" pink cotton (backing)

(1) 14" x 16 ½" pale pink cotton (inner panel)

16" cushion insert

# STEPS

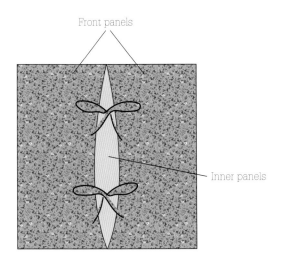

Front panels

Inner panels

1 Take one of the 1 ½" x 14" strips for the ties, fold one short edge in by ¼", wrong sides facing, and press. Fold a long edge in by ¼" in and press, then repeat for the other long edge. Fold the strip in two lengthways, wrong sides facing, and press. Top stitch the folded sides. Repeat for the other three tie strips.

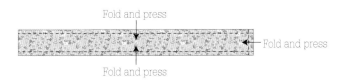

Fold and press

Fold and press

Fold and press

2 Take a pink lining piece, mark two spots along one long edge at 5", 6 ½" and 5" intervals as shown. Place a tie on top of each mark and baste or pin in place. Place a pink floral rectangle on top, RST, and sew together along the long edge with the ties. Press the seam open, fold the lining to the other side of the floral fabric and press again. Top stitch the edge with the ties. Make two. These are the two front panels for the cushion.

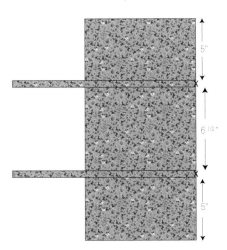

5"

6 ½"

5"

3 Take the pale pink inner panel, fold one long edge in by 1", press. Fold in by another inch and press. Top stitch the folded edge.

4 Place the backing fabric on a flat surface, right side facing up. Place the two front panels on top, raw edges aligned and floral side facing down. Finally place the inner panel on top, right side facing down. Pin together and sew all the way around.

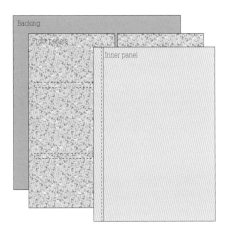

Backing

Front panels

Inner panel

5 Clip the corners and turn inside out through the opening on one side of the inner panel. Place the cushion insert inside.

# 'TAKE ME HOME' QUILT

The design of this quilt reminded me of a flock of birds, flying towards 'home'. It's a beginner - friendly classic quilt that is simple to piece, and will add a splash of colour to any room.

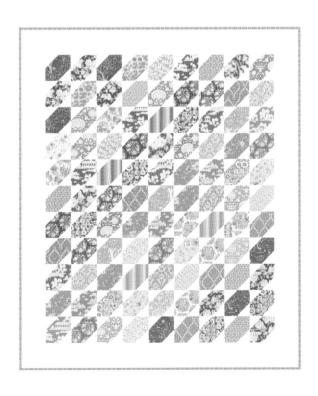

Size: 66" x 78"

# NOTES

Finished size: 66" x 78"

RST means right sides together

Use a ¼" seam allowance unless otherwise stated

WOF means width of fabric (based on a standard bolt that is 42" wide)

Refer to 'Techniques' for more guidance on quilting methods

# MATERIALS

(99) 6 ½" print squares in a mix of rainbow colours

(198) 3 ½" white squares

(8) 6 ½" 33 ½" white strips for borders

(2) 72" x WOF backing

(1) 72" x 84" batting

(7) 2 ¼" x WOF strips for binding

# STEPS

1  Using a fabric marker draw a diagonal line from one corner to the opposite corner on the back of the white 3 ½" squares.

2  To make a quilt block, place a white square RST on one corner of a 6 ½ " print square, as shown. Sew on the traced line. Place another white square on the opposite corner and repeat. Trim excess fabric ¼" away from the seam, fold the seam open, press towards the white.

3  Repeat step 2 to make 99 blocks in assorted rainbow colours.

4  Stack the finished blocks in colour order (e.g. starting with purple, then blues, then greens and so on). Lay out your blocks on a flat surface in a 9 x 11 grid - starting on one corner and laying them out in diagonals towards the opposite corner to achieve a rainbow graduated effect.

5  Sew together the nine blocks in each row, pressing seams in alternate directions (e.g. top row to the left, second row to the right, and so on).

6  Sew the rows together, making sure you pin the seams at each intersection well. They should nest together nicely as the seams were pressed in alternate directions. Press the seams between each row open.

7  Sew the white border strips together in pairs along a short edge to get four 66 ½" long strips. Sew two of these strips to the right and left of the quilt centre. Press seams towards white. Sew the two other strips to the top and bottom. Press seams towards white.

8  Sew the two backing pieces together along one long edge. Press seam open.

9  Lay out your backing fabric on a hard floor right side facing down, making sure it's completely smooth. Put masking tape along each edge to secure it down if necessary.

10  Lay the batting over the top, then your quilt top, right side facing up. Baste the three layers together with quilting pins.

11  Quilt the three layers together as desired. Trim the excess backing fabric and batting.

12  Sew your binding strips together with diagonal seams to get one long strip. Press the binding strip in half, wrong sides facing. Sew the binding onto the quilt (see 'Techniques' for guidance).

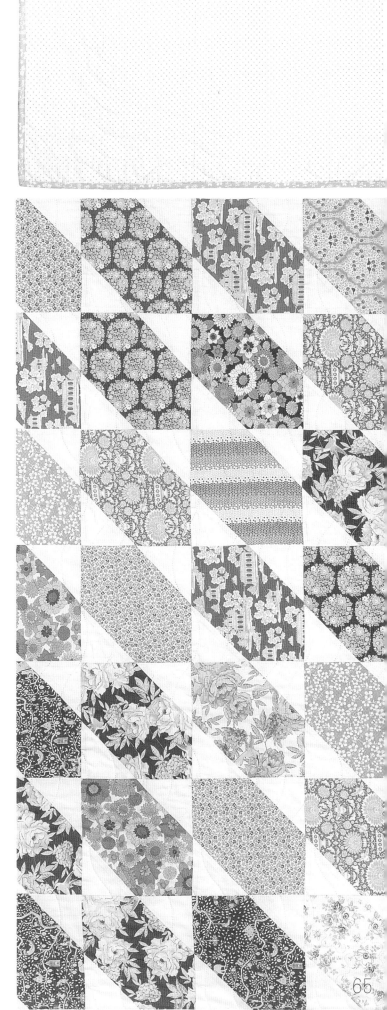

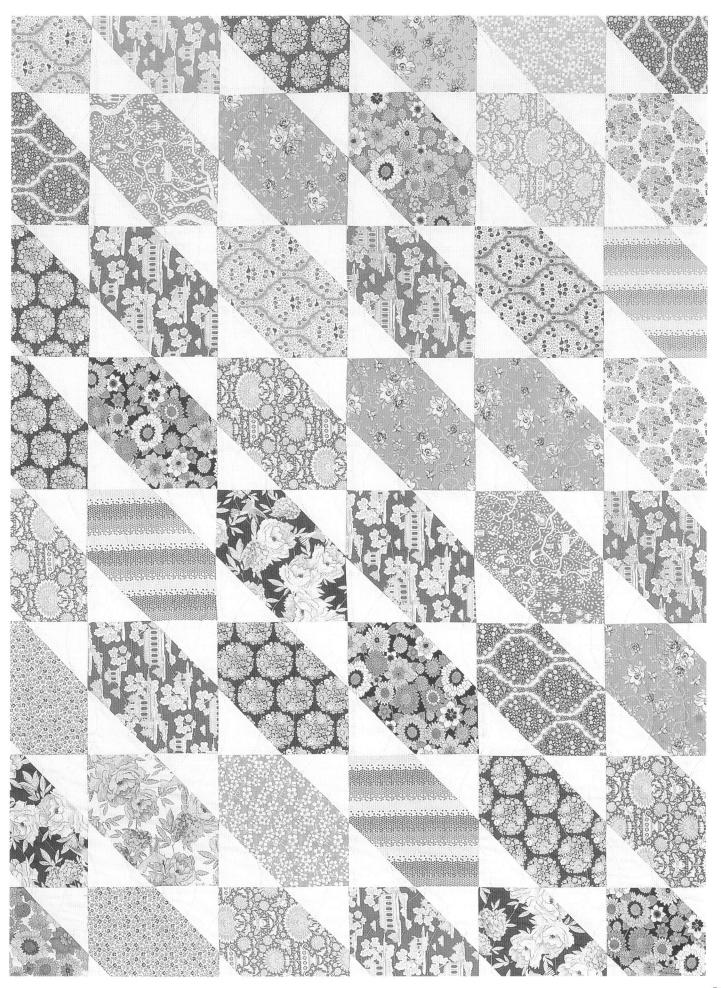

# THE ULTIMATE PINCUSHION

This jumbo sized pincushion is large enough to house all your pins, and deep enough for those extra long ones too!

Size: 6" x 6" x 1.5"

# NOTES

Finished size: 6" x 6" x 1.5"

RST means right sides together

Use a ¼" seam allowance unless otherwise stated

# MATERIALS

(8) 4" x 4" assorted print fabrics (pincushion top)

(8) 4" x 4" fusible web (pincushion top)

(1) 7" x 7" fabric in a neutral colour (pincushion top)

(4) 6 ½" x 1 ¾" assorted print fabrics (pincushion sides)

(2) 6 ½" x 3 ½" rectangles (pincushion bottom)

(1) Large wood button

Crushed walnut shells or fiber fill (filling)

# STEPS

1. Apply fusible web to the wrong side of the 4" square prints following the manufacturer's instructions.

2. Place template 1 on the paper backing of four of the 4" square pieces and trace around. Cut out on the line. Repeat with template 2 on the remaining four 4" square pieces.

3. Draw a 6" square in the middle of the 7" square fabric. Peel back the paper on the appliqué shapes, place them inside the 6" square as shown, fuse in place with iron.

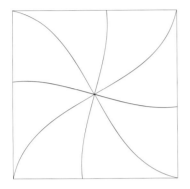

4. Using a small zigzag setting on your machine stitch the seams between the appliqué shapes and all the way around the 6" square.

5. Trim ¼" outside the perimeter of the appliqué square to make a 6 ½" square.

6. Place two of the side rectangles RST and sew together along one short edge, leaving ¼" unstitched at the top and bottom. Repeat for the remaining side rectangles until you have a loop of all four side rectangles. Press seams open.

7. Pin one side rectangle to the pincushion top, RST. Sew together, leaving ¼" unstitched at both ends. Repeat for the remaining side rectangles until the loop is sewn onto the pincushion top.

8. Place the two bottom rectangles RST and sew along one long edge, leaving a 3" gap in the middle (make sure you secure beginning and end stitches well). Press the seam open.

9. Repeat step 7 to sew the sides to the bottom. Turn inside out through the opening.

10. Stuff the pincushion firmly through the opening. Blind stitch the seam closed by hand.

11. Sew the wood button in the middle, going all the way through the pincushion and back up again several times. This is not only a decorative touch but also helps stabilise the pincushion so that it sits flat.

# VERSATILE DRAWSTRING BAG

You can find many uses for this versatile bag around your home - as a laundry bag, a pyjama bag, or to keep soft toys tidy.

Size: 17.5" x 21"

# MATERIALS

(10) 4" x 21 ½ " strips in assorted print fabrics (bag outer)

(2) 18" x 21 ½" white cotton (lining)

(2) 2 ¼"  x 2 ½" print fabric (tab)

(1) 2 ¼"  x 2 ½" batting (tab)

(1) 20" x 45" batting

2 metres of 8mm rope or cord

10 extra large grommets

# STEPS

1 Make the bag outer. Organise the strips into two blocks of 5. Sew 5 strips in one block together along their long edges. Press seams open. Repeat with the remaining strips. Sew the two blocks together along one short edge. Press the seam open.

2 Draw two lines 2" from the top and bottom of the bag outer. Place on top of the batting and pin all over (the batting will be larger). Sew along the two traced lines at the top and bottom. Quilt the centre section between these two lines as desired. Trim off excess batting.

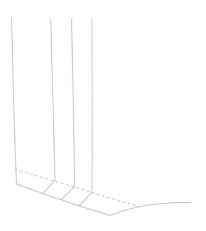

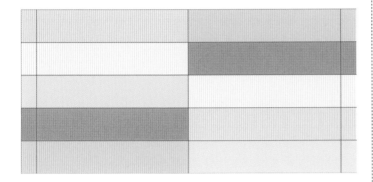

3 Sew the two lining pieces together, leaving a 6" gap in the middle for turning inside out. Secure beginning and end stitches on either side of the gap well. Press seam open.

4 Place the lining on top of the quilted bag front, RST. Trim off any excess fabric if the lining and the bag front aren't exactly the same size. Sew along both short edges.

5 Fold the bag so that the two lining pieces lie against each other and the two quilted bag front pieces against each other. Sew along both long edges. Cut out a 1 ½" square from all four corners as shown.

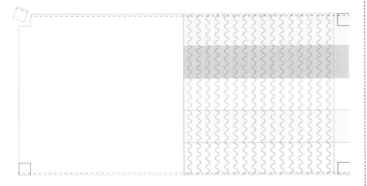

6 Make the corner tab. Place both tab rectangles RST and place on top of the little batting piece. Sew along three edges, leaving a short edge open. Clip the corners, turn inside out. Following manufacturer's instructions install a grommet in the centre.

7 Open the seam at one corner cut out and fold the other way so the two opposite seams meet. Insert the corner tab through the gap, raw edge aligned with the raw edges of fabric and the sewn edge facing inwards towards the bag. Sew all the way across to 'box' the corner. Repeat the same process for the other three corners (these have no tabs).

8 Turn the bag inside out through the opening in the lining. Blind stitch the opening closed by hand. Push the lining inside the bag, poking it into the corners.

9 Press the top edge of the bag and top stitch all the way around.

10 Install a grommet on each 'stripe' above the stitch line that's 2" down from the bag's top edge.

11 Starting in a grommet next to the side seam on the opposite side from the tab, knot the thread on the inside of the bag and start threading the rope through the grommets, in and out. When you get to the end of the first side of the bag go down and thread the rope through the tab grommet, back up again and through the first grommet on the other side. Keep threading the rope through the grommets and finish with a knot on the inside of the last grommet. Cut off any excess rope.

# KITTY & TEDDY KEY RINGS

My son drew this kitty and teddy when he was only 5 years old, and I wanted to make something sweet with them ever since. Use them as key rings, or add a lobster clip to make the cutest bag charms!

Size: 4" square (including tab)

# MATERIALS

For each key ring:

(2) 5" x 5" wool felt squares (backing)

(1) 4" square linen (face)

(1) 2" square print fabric (ears and muzzle)

(1) 1" square fabric (nose)

(1) 1" square pink felt (tongue)

(1) 5" square piece of fusible web

(1) 3" cotton tape or ribbon for the tag

(1) key ring

Black thread and thread matching the colour of your felt backing

Polyester fibre fill

## STEPS

1 Apply fusible web to the back of the fabrics for the face, ears, muzzle and nose. Trace the templates provided for each piece onto the paper backing and cut them out. (See Techniques for 'Raw Edge Applique')

2 Place the face piece in the middle of one felt square and fuse in place by pressing with hot iron (Tip: If using acrylic felt instead of wool felt, cover with a cloth before pressing). Place the muzzle, ears, and nose on top of the face and fuse in place. Using a fabric pen mark where the eyes will be (and whiskers for the cat).

3 Thread your machine with the black thread for the top thread and the other thread matching your felt for the bobbin thread. Using a short stitch length sew around the edges of each of the applique pieces twice. A little imperfection is actually good here as it creates a thicker line and gives a 'hand drawn' feel. Go over the eyes a few times until you are happy with the thickness of your line.

4 Trim excess felt all the way around a few mm away from the face fabric.

5 Cut out the pink felt tongue using the template. Sew a black line through the middle of the tongue as shown, going over it a few times (Tip: Place the tongue on top of a piece of paper and sew through the felt and paper to stabilise the felt. You can then rip the paper off once you've finished sewing)

6 Place the face on top of the other square of felt. Thread the ring through the cotton tape, fold in two and place on the top edge of the face, with ¼" of the tape lying underneath the face. Pin. Do the same for the tongue under the nose. Sew over the outer perimeter of the face in black thread one more time, starting on one side of the face and leaving a 1" gap. Lightly stuff with fibre fill. Finish sewing the perimeter with black thread, closing the gap.

7 Trim the excess felt on the back close to the edge. Take care with the tape and tongue – flip these to the other side to make sure you don't cut them by mistake.

# FLORAL DOORSTOP

These doorstops are ideal for propping
open doors and adding a splash of colour to
any room. They make lovely housewarming
gifts too!

Size: 5 ½" x 7" (including handle)

# MATERIALS

For each doorstop:

(1) 8" x 18" floral duck / canvas (sides)

(1) 5" square floral duck / canvas (top)

(1) 5 ½" x 7" floral duck / canvas (bottom)

(1) 6 ½" 7" floral duck / canvas (bottom)

(2) 2" x 5 ½" rectangles (handle)

(2) Large wood buttons

(1) 4 ½" strip of Velcro

Upholstery thread or DMC Cotton Perle No 8

Rice or sand to fill

# STEPS

1 Copy part A and part B of the template onto paper and tape them together along the edges marked with the arrows. Place onto the side fabric, trace around and cut the shape out on the line. Fold in two RST, pin and sew along the raw edge. Press seam open. Fold in two so the seam lies to one side. Finger press the top and bottom edge on the opposite side to the seam, and mark these spots with a fabric pen. Now fold in two again so these marks lie against the seam. Finger press the top and bottom edges on both sides, and mark these spots with a fabric pen. You have now marked the four quarters of both the top and bottom edge of your side fabric.

2 Trace the circle for the top of the doorstop onto the 5" square fabric and cut out on the line. Fold in two right sides facing, finger press the top and bottom edges. Open and mark these spots. Fold again in two matching the marks from the previous step, finger press, and mark these spots. You have now marked the four quarters of the top of the doorstop.

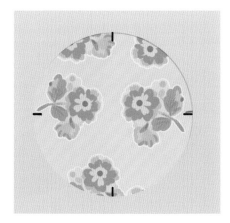

3 Fold one long edge of one of the bottom pieces in by 1" and press. Fold again by another inch and press. Top stitch along the folded edge. Repeat for the other bottom piece.

4 Centre the 'hook' part of the Velcro on the edge of the larger bottom piece on the 'right' side of the fabric, stitch all the way around twice securing it well. Sew the 'loop' part of the Velcro on the edge of the smaller bottom piece on the 'wrong' side, and sew in place.

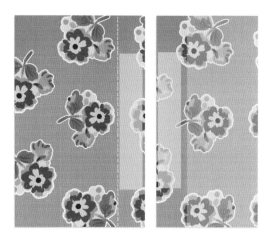

5 Align and press the two Velcro pieces together. Place the bottom circle template on top, aligning two of the central guides on the template with the edge of the central opening, and trace all the way around. To keep the central opening closed, sew two little stitches a few mm from the edge on the inside of the traced circle. Place the template on top again and carefully mark the two side points where the template guides are. These two marks and the edge of the central opening marks the four quadrants of the bottom of the doorstop. Cut the circle shape out on the traced line.

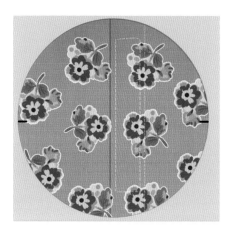

83

6 Pin the top circle to the top edge of the doorstop sides, starting by aligning and pinning the four quadrant marks first (this will make sure the fabric is distributed evenly and won't bunch up). Sew all the way around ¼" from the edge, making sure the fabric is not stretched or pinched at any point.

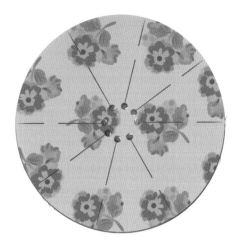

7 Repeat the previous step for the bottom of the doorstop. Turn inside out through the opening at the bottom and poke out the edges with a blunt instrument or turning tool.

8 To make the handle place the two 2" x 5 ½" strips RST and sew all the way around leaving a 1 ½" gap. Clip the corners and turn inside out through the gap. Tuck in the seam allowance at the opening and press. Top stitch all the way around a few mm from the edge. Sew to the top of the doorstop with wood buttons using a thick thread such as upholstery thread or cotton perle.

9 Make a funnel out of paper and fill the doorstop with rice or sand. Secure the Velcro at the bottom.

# STAR TABLE TOPPER

A pretty table topper is the ultimate finishing touch for a well decorated table, and this one really steals the show with its unusual star shape. Try making it in high contrast fabrics to make the pattern stand out.

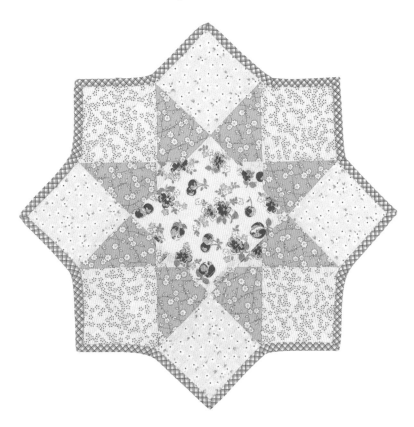

Size: 14.5" square

# NOTES

Finished size: 14 ½" square

RST means right sides together

Use a ¼" seam allowance unless otherwise stated

Refer to 'Techniques' for guidance on patchwork and quilting

# MATERIALS

(1) 5" x 5" cherry floral

(8) 1 ¼" x 1 ¼" cherry floral

(8) 2 ¾" x 3 ½" green floral

(4) 3 ½" x 3 ½" light green floral

(2) 3 ¾" x 3 ¾" cream floral

(8) 2 ¾" x 2 ¾" cream floral

(1) 16" x 16" backing fabric

(1) 16" x 16" batting

(1) 2 ¼" x 60" binding

## PATCHWORK DIAGRAM

# STEPS

1  Trace a diagonal line from corner to corner on the back of the 1 ¼" cherry floral and 2 ¾" cream floral squares.

2  Place a cream floral on the left side of a 2 ¾" x 3 ½" green floral, RST and with the traced diagonal running from the left bottom corner to the top of the green floral rectangle. Sew along the traced line and trim ¼" away from the seam. Flip open and press seam towards the triangle. Sew the 1 ¼" square in the same manner on the top right hand side, trim and press towards the triangle. Make 4.

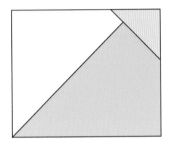

3  Using the same method make four units that are mirror images of the units from the previous step. Start with sewing the large square on the right side, then sew the small square on the left side.

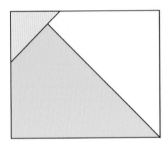

4  Refer to the patchwork diagram to see how the top will be pieced together. To start, pair a unit from step 2 with a unit from step 3 and sew together as shown. Press seam open. Make 4.

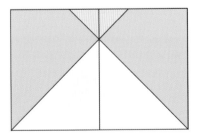

5  Sew each of the three rows together as shown. Press the seams towards the light green squares in the first and third rows and towards the central cherry floral in the second row.

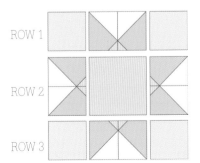

ROW 1

ROW 2

ROW 3

6  Sew the three rows together, nesting and pinning the seams at each intersection. Press these two seams open.

7  Cut the two 3 ¾" squares in half diagonally, yielding four triangles. Take a triangle, fold it in half right sides facing and finger press to mark the centre. Open and place RST on the top middle of the patchwork, lining the finger pressed central fold with the central seam. Sew across. Flip open and press towards the triangle. Repeat for the other three edges.

8  Make a quilt sandwich with the backing fabric, batting, and patchwork top. Quilt as desired. Trim off excess backing and batting. (see Techniques)

9  Press the binding strip in half lengthways, wrong sides facing together. Bind the table topper, mitring the 90 degree corners (see Techniques). To bind an inside corner, clip each inside corner with a very scant ¼" with small scissors. As you sew your binding to the quilt, when you approach each inside corner mark a point ¼" away from the edge as shown. This is your pivot point. Sew all the way to the pivot point and stop with the needle down. Lift the presser foot and pull the quilt to straighten the edge, so it forms a straight line before and after the needle. Continue sewing the binding. This method will gently ease the binding around an inside corner.

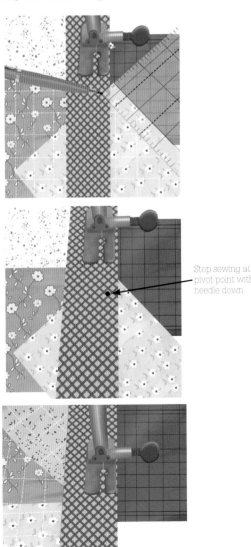

Stop sewing at pivot point with needle down

# SWEET POUCHES

Sweet and functional, these zakka pouches are the perfect size to store all your odds and ends and they make lovely little gift bags too!

Size: 5" x 8"

# MATERIALS

(2) 5 ½" square floral print fabric

(2) 3 ¾" x 5 ½" white linen

(2) 5 ½" x 8 ½" lining fabric

(1) 40" piece of suede cord

(1) Suede tassel

(2) Wooden beads

# STEPS

1 Fold one floral piece in half right sides facing, and finger press the top edge to mark the centre. Open. Cut a 2 ½" piece of cord, thread it through the hole in the tassel, fold the cord in half, and machine baste in place where the finger pressed centre mark is, 1/8" away from the edge.

2 Place a white linen rectangle on top RST, sew together along the top edge. Open and press the seam towards the white linen. Place a lining rectangle on top of the white linen RST, sew together along the top edge. Press seam open. This is the front of the pouch. Repeat to make the back of the pouch (without a tassel).

3 Trace and cut out the 2" circle template provided. Place the template on a corner, trace around, and cut along the traced line. Repeat for all four corners. This will give the pouch slightly rounded corners at the bottom.

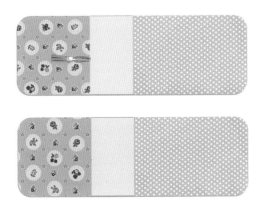

4 Place the front and back pieces RST, aligning the lining pieces, the white linen, and the floral. Pin together, making sure the seams are lying precisely against each other. Using a fabric marker mark a 2" gap on the short edge of the lining piece, also place small marks on both side edges 2" and 2 ½" down from the seam between the white linen and the lining (these mark the location of the cord casing). Sew all the way around, leaving the gaps unsewn. When sewing secure all beginning and end stitches well by sewing back and forth a few times. Clip the corners with pinking shears.

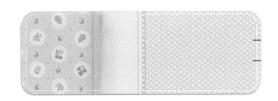

5 Turn the pouch inside out through the 2" gap. Push out the corners with a blunt instrument or turning tool. Carefully press the pouch, making sure the seams on all sides are lying flat. Tuck in the seam allowance at the opening by ¼" as well and press it.

6 Blind stitch the opening closed by hand (see 'Techniques'). Push the lining into the bag, press the edge for a neat finish.

7 You will next top stitch the top edge of the bag and the cord casing. Mark lines on both sides of the bag 1/8" from the top, 2" from the top and 2 ½" from the top. Carefully top stitch all the way around these lines making sure you are only stitching one side of the pouch at a time and you aren't sewing through all layers. This will require you to stop frequently and reposition the pouch. When sewing the two lower stitch lines fold out the edge of the pouch as shown to make it easier to manipulate the pouch on your sewing machine.

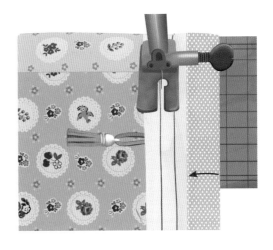

8 Cut the remaining cord in half. Take one half and using a safety pin carefully thread it through the cord casing, starting on one side, going all the way around the bag and coming out again on the same side. Repeat with the other half, starting and finishing on the other side of the pouch. Pull and adjust the cord ends until they are all the same length. Thread the cord ends on one side through a wooden bead, tie a knot at the end and cut off the excess cord. Repeat for the other side.

# 'BLOOM'
# WALL ART

What better way to adorn a blank wall than with this pretty
floral wall art? The three dimensional applique petals and leaves
of this mini quilt makes it a real conversation piece.

Size: 14 ½" x 18 ½"

# NOTES

Finished size: 14 ½" x 18 ½"

RST means right sides together

Use a ¼" seam allowance unless otherwise stated.

# MATERIALS

(2) 18" x 22" ivory cotton (front and backing)

(1) 18" x 22" batting

(10) 2 ½" square pink cotton (petals)

(10) 2 ½" square white cotton (petals)

(8) 2 ½" square pale pink cotton (petals)

(16) 2" x 4" green cotton (leaves)

(3) 2" square scraps in grey, white, and yellow (flower centres)

(1) 2" square lilac cotton (berries)

(1) 2" square fusible web (berries)

(2) 2 ½" x 30" strips cut on the bias (binding)

Sewing thread in colours one shade darker than your petals, leaves, and berries

Fibre fill

# STEPS

1 Assemble the template by taping the sections of the pattern together. Using a window or light box trace the outline of the oval, and the flowers, petals and berries onto the front fabric.

2 Make a quilt sandwich with the front fabric, the batting, and backing. Quilt as desired (see 'Techniques' for more guidance on this step).

3 To make the leaves, trace the leaf template onto the back of a green rectangle. Place RST with another green rectangle and sew along the traced line all the way around. Trim excess fabric all the way around with pinking shears. Using sharp pointy scissors make a small + shaped slit on the back, being careful not to cut through the front of the leaf. Turn inside out through the slit, poke the edges and points out with a blunt instrument, press. Repeat to make 8 leaves.

4 By hand draw some random vein patterns on each leaf. Place each leaf on the quilted background, and sew in place using green top thread and ivory bobbin thread, going over each line twice.

5 Repeat the same process to make all the petals and sew them in place with coordinating top thread.

6 Following the manufacturer's instructions apply fusible web to the back of the lilac square. Trace the berry template onto the paper backing five times, and cut out the five berries. Peel off the backing paper and press to fuse in place on the background. Sew all the way around each berry with a short zigzag stitch.

7 Make the flower centres using same method as step 3. Place them in the middle of each flower, appliqué stitch by machine or hand all the way around, leaving a ½" gap on one side. Stuff a small amount of fibre fill through the gap to make the centvre lightly padded. Continue to appliqué stitch to close the gap.

8 Cut off the excess fabric and batting along the oval outline. Join the binding strips together with diagonal seams. Press in half lengthways, wrong sides facing together. Bind the mini quilt, using quilting clips to gently ease the binding around the curved edge (see 'Techniques' for guidance on binding). (Tip: it is important to use binding strips that are cut on the 'bias' as this ensures the binding goes around the curved edge more easily, without distortion).

# BENTO BAG

'Bento' is a Japanese term meaning a packed lunch or snack, which is typically carried in a compact bag that can be tied at the top. This versatile little bag can also be used as gift packaging - try filling it with freshly baked cookies and gift it to a loved one!

Size: 6" x 5" x 3" (excluding ties)

# MATERIALS

(1) 9" x 14 ½" floral (outer)

(1) 9" x 14 ½" batting

(2) 7 ½" x 9" pink cotton (lining)

(2) 3 ½" x 10" floral (ties)

(2) 3 ½" x 10" pink cotton (ties)

(2) 6" pieces of 3/8" elastic

# STEPS

1 Sew the two lining pieces together along one short edge, leaving a 4" gap in the middle unsewn. Press the seam open.

2 Place the floral outer on top of the batting, right side facing up. Place the lining on top, right side facing down. Pin together.

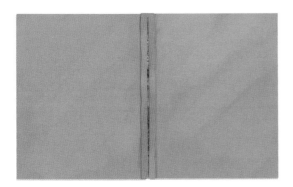

3 Sew the two short edges with a ¼" seam. Turn inside out so the right sides of the floral and the lining are facing outwards. Press the sewn edges, and trace a line ½" away from the edge on both sides. Sew a straight line across the traced lines, thus creating two channels or casings at either end of the bag. Using a safety pin thread an elastic through these casings and sew the elastic in place at either end 1/8" away from the edge.

4 Turn the bag inside out again so the wrong sides of the lining and the batting are facing outwards. Fold the bag so that the two lining pieces lie against each other and the two batting/floral pieces against each other. Sew across both long edges. Cut out a 1 ½" square piece from each of the four corners.

5 Open the seam at one corner cut out and fold the other way so the two opposite seams meet. Sew all the way across to 'box' the corner. Repeat the same process for the other three corners.

6 Turn the bag inside out through the gap in the lining. Blind stitch the opening closed by hand. Push the lining inside the bag, poking it into the corners.

7 Trace the tie template onto the wrong side of the two floral tie strips. Place RST with a pink strip and sew across both sides and the curved edge of the tie, leaving the short straight edge unsewn. Trim off excess fabric with pinking scissors. Turn inside out through the opening on the short edge, push out the edges of the fabric with a blunt instrument. Tuck in the seam by ¼" on the unsewn edge and press. Blind stitch the opening closed by hand. Repeat to make the other tie.

8 Place a tie on the inside top edge of one of the sides of the bag, centred on the side seam. The tie should overlap the side of the bag by ½" with the curved edge of the tie pointing up and the floral side facing outwards. Pin, and sew a straight line across the bottom edge of the tie and another line a few mm from the top edge of the bag to secure the tie in place. Repeat with the other tie on the other side of the bag.

# ORIGAMI
# MARKET TOTE

This tote was inspired by 'origami' - the ancient Japanese art of paper folding. The front section of this very spacious market bag can be folded and secured with cord ties for a different look.

Size: 14" x 23"

# MATERIALS

(1) 23 ½" x 28 ½" outer fabric

(1) 23 ½" x 28 1/2" batting

(2) 14 ½" x 23 ½" lining fabric

(6) Large grommets

(1) Magnetic bag snap

70" 14mm rope or cord

15" 9mm rope or cord

# STEPS

**1** Sew the two lining pieces together along one long edge, leaving a 6" gap in the middle for turning inside out. Secure beginning and end stitches on either side of the gap well. Press the seam open.

**2** Place quilt outer on top of the batting, right side up. Place the lining on top, RST. Sew across the short edges on either end.

**3** Fold the bag so that the two lining pieces lie against each other and the two front pieces (with the batting) lie against each other. Sew along both long edges.

**4** Cut out a 2 ½" square from all four corners. Open the seam at one corner cut out and fold the other way so the two opposite seams meet. Sew all the way across to 'box' the corner. Repeat the same process for the other three corners.

**5** Turn the bag inside out through the opening in the lining. Mark the centre of the bag on the lining 1 inch below the top edge. Insert magnetic bag snaps following the manufacturer's instructions (you can reach into the inner part of the bag through the opening in the lining). Blind stitch the opening closed by hand and push the lining inside.

**6** Top stitch the top edge of the bag all the way around, approximately 3/8" from the edge.

**7** Install two grommets along the top edge of one side of the bag, 8" away from the outer corners and with the centre of each grommet 1" away from the top edge. There should be a gap of 7" between the grommets (centre to centre). Repeat to add two grommets to the other side of the bag.

**8** On one side of the bag, add two grommets to the two outer top corners, an inch away from both edges. These are for the cord ties when the bag front is folded.

**9** Insert the thick rope into the top central grommets, knotting the ends on the inside. Each handle should be ~26" long (you can adjust the length of the handles according to your personal preference). Cut the excess rope.

**10** Insert the ends of the thin rope through the outer corner grommets, knot in the middle to gather the bag corners to the middle of the bag. Make a knot at either end of the rope, leaving a 3" piece of rope at both ends. Open up the threads of the 3" excess ropes on either end and gently brush with a hairbrush to form a tassel. Trim the tassel ends even.

# TEMPLATES

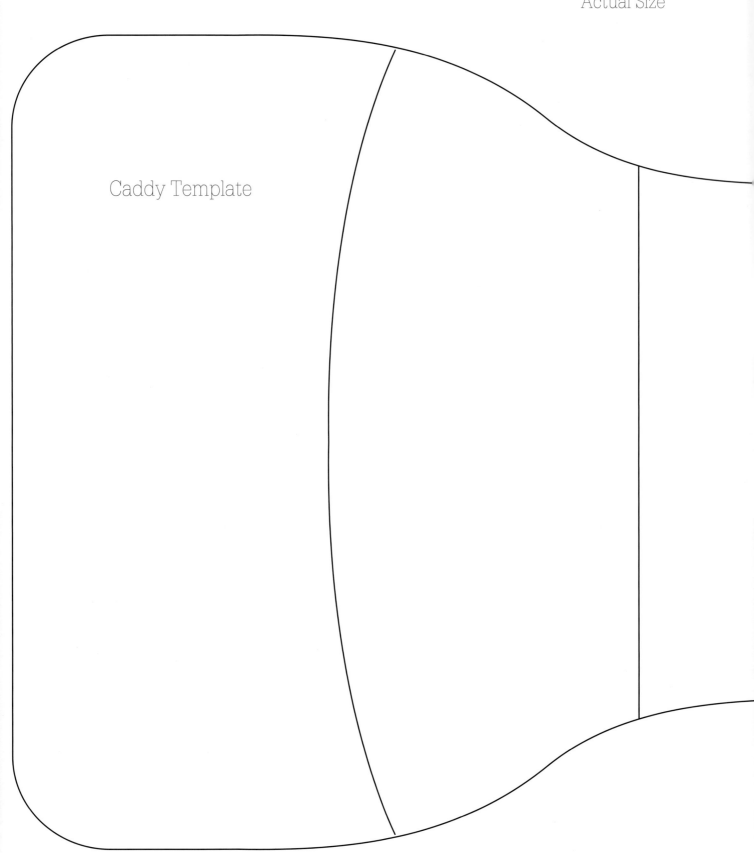

Caddy Template

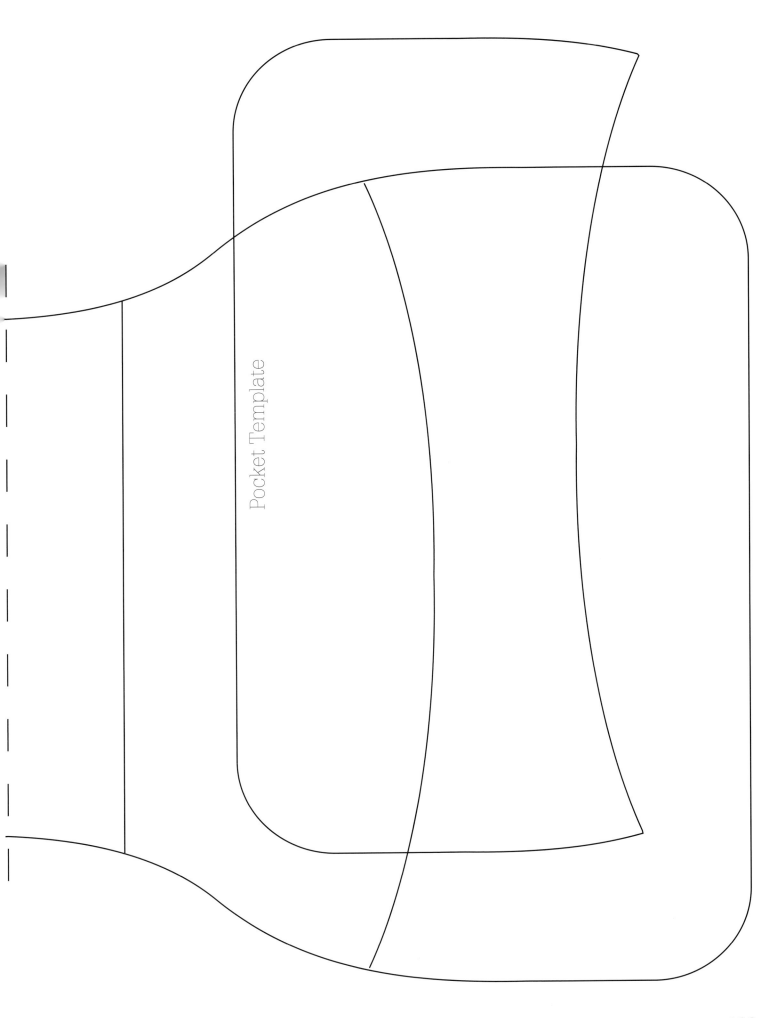

Pocket Template

# HOUSE LAVENDER SACHETS
## PAGE 32

Actual Size

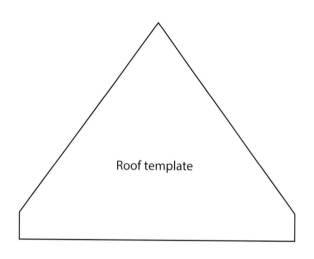

Roof template

# BOUQUET EMBROIDERY
## PAGE 28

Actual Size

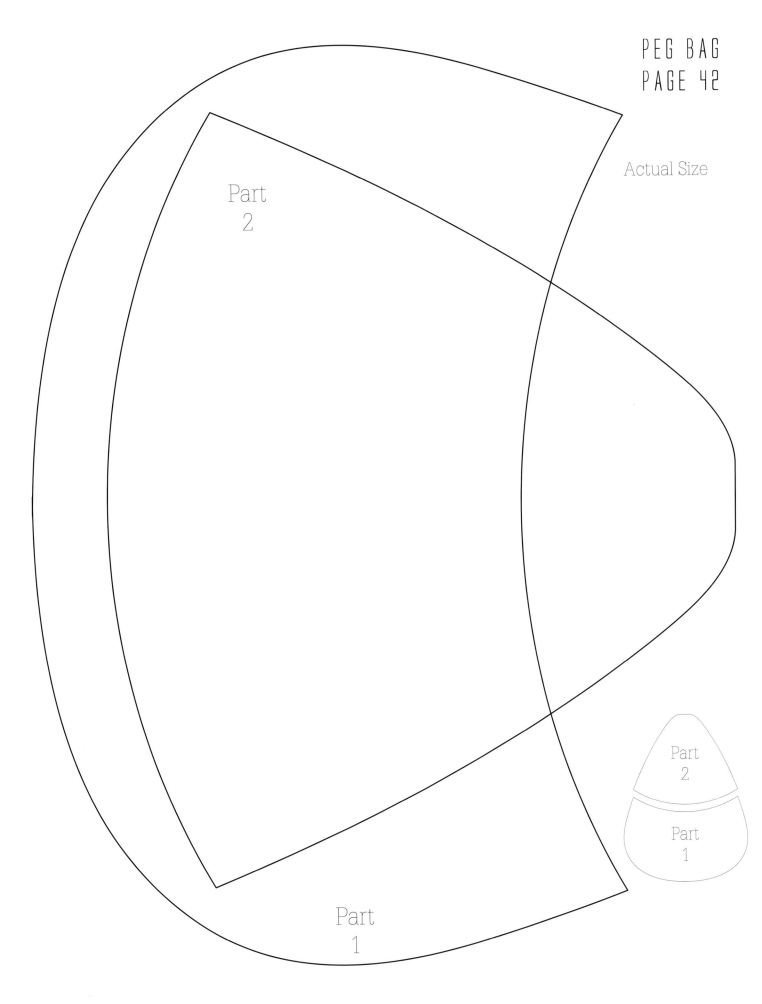

PEG BAG
PAGE 42

Actual Size

Part
2

Part
1

Part
2

Part
1

# SASHIKO COASTERS
## PAGE 50

Actual Size

Actual Size

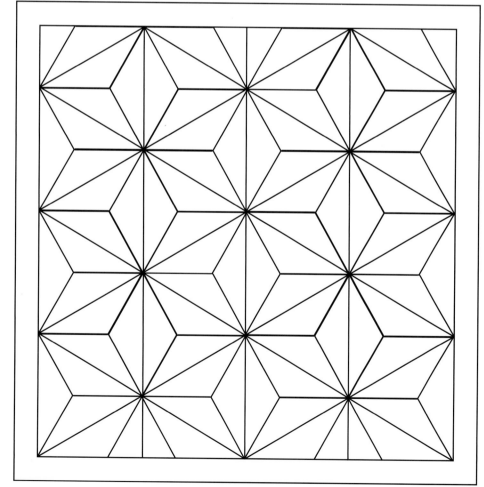

Actual Size

Actual Size

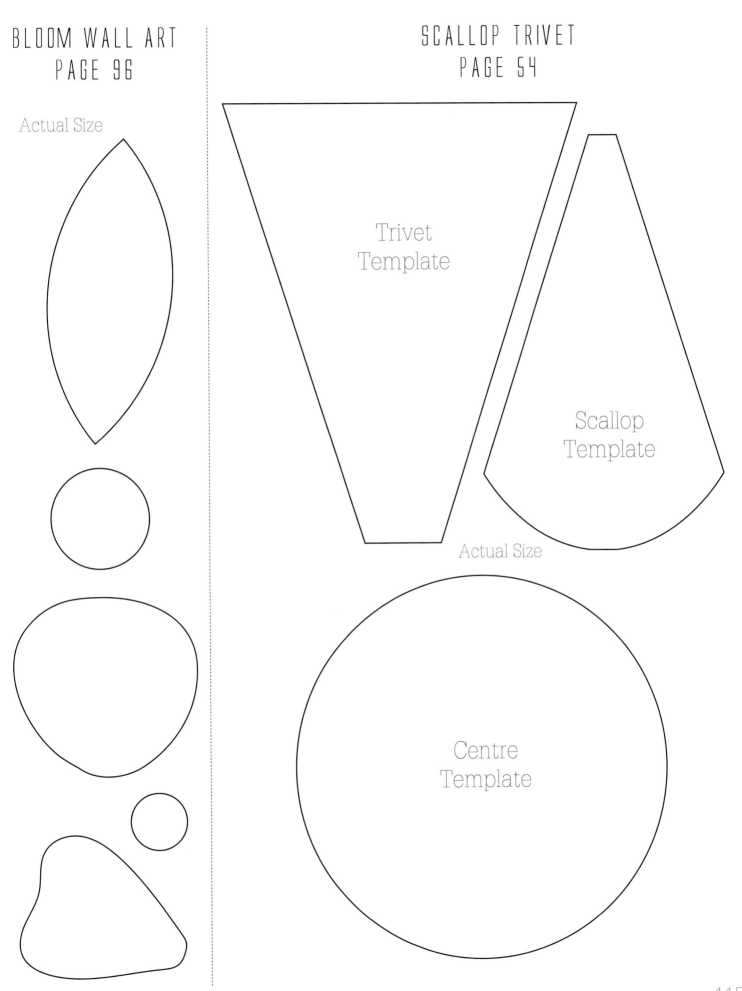

BLOOM WALL ART
PAGE 96

Actual Size

SCALLOP TRIVET
PAGE 54

Trivet
Template

Scallop
Template

Actual Size

Centre
Template

115

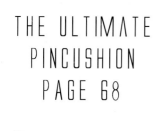

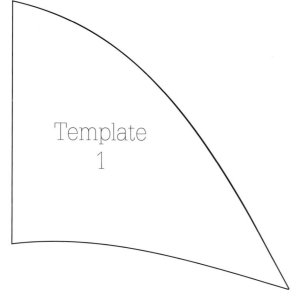

Template
1

Actual Size

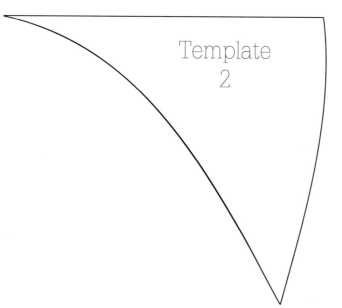

Template
2

Actual Size

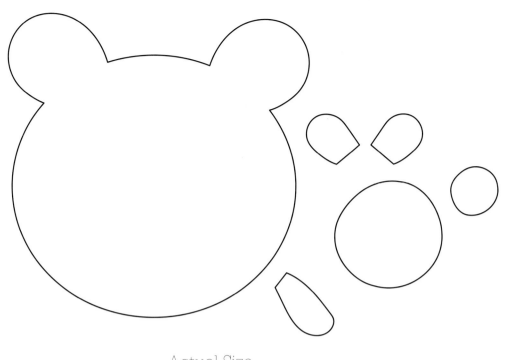

Actual Size

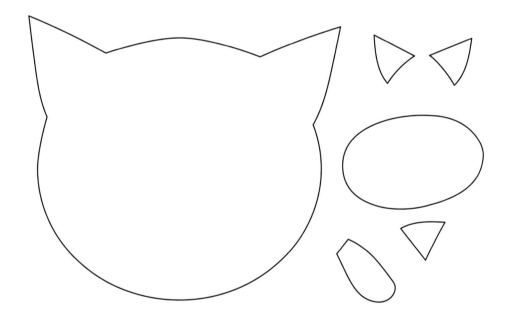

SWEET POUCHES
PAGE 90

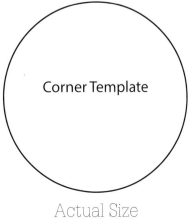

Corner Template

Actual Size

# FLORAL DOORSTOP
## PAGE 80

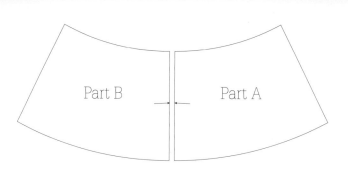

Part B | Part A

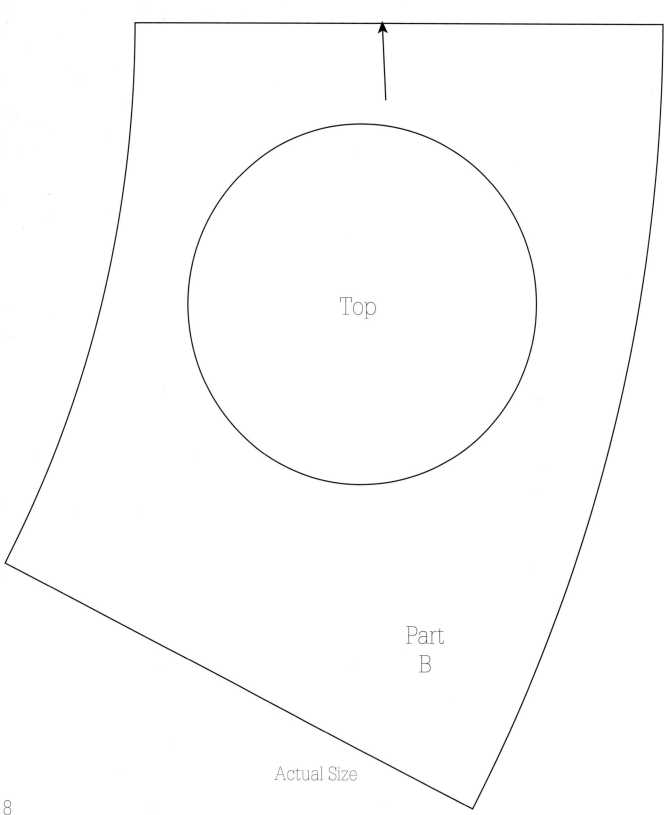

Top

Part
B

Actual Size

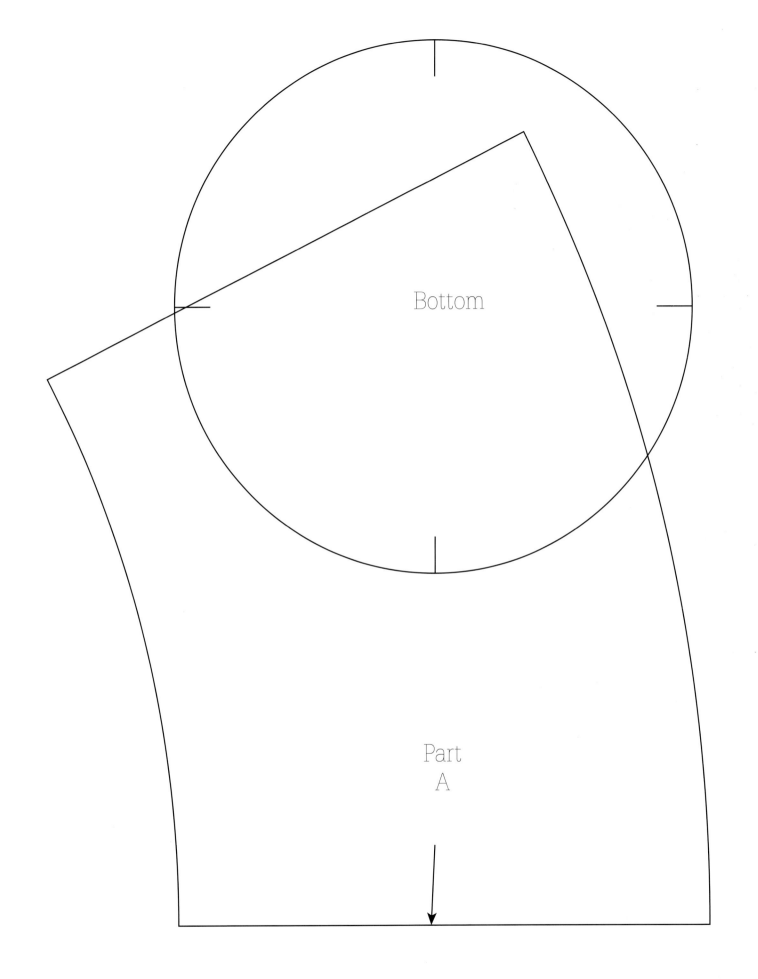

Bottom

Part
A

Actual Size